Walking Off the Land

First published 2021 by The Hedgehog Poetry Press

Published in the UK by
The Hedgehog Poetry Press
5, Coppack House
Churchill Avenue
Clevedon
BS21 6QW

www.hedgehogpress.co.uk

ISBN: 978-1-913499-38-9

9 8 7 6 5 4 3 2 1

A CIP Catalogue record for this book is available from the
British Library.

Printed and bound By TJ Books Limited

Walking Off the Land

by

Anne McMaster

Contents

In loving memory of my parents

Jeannie Workman McMaster: 1920 -1994

William Robert (Wilbert) McMaster: 1918 -1995

SILVER

These roads were horse tracks once,
curving slowly into a rising hill,
easing the passage of harvest-heavy carts
hauled by teams of horses to each quiet farm,
their sweating heads held low, necks taut,
as their hooves spat sound, ice-sharp,
into a darkening sky.

I'm told that highwaymen roamed here too,
their cache still buried in the fields above the farm.
So, when I walk these shadowed roads in winter
and the moon is all I have,
my thoughts are now of silver.
The cool wash of moonlight across a sour and empty hedge,
wheels sliding deep into an inked slick, mud-thick brae,
eyes gleaming, wet with fear, at a sudden dark interruption.
The glint of silver at a horse's foaming mouth.

HOME AT THE RANGE

There were no pretensions to fashion where I lived.
Farmers worked hard –
rearing children, crops and (sometimes) smiles.
Farmhouses tended toward practicality. Utility.
No technicolour visions of a stage Irish dream.
Ranges were the hearts that beat in every house;
practical little beasts – the pit ponies of fire –
no thoroughbred Agas here.
A stalwart Rayburn or a Belling would heat your water for you,
dry your clothes and cook your food.
The range here at the farm gave up after ninety years of use.
Friends – both strong and brave of heart – stripped it down and laid it bare;
three quarters of a ton of iron and steel.
I mourned its loss as though a friend had died.
It had been the centre of our family life.
My mother roasted stews that were thick and dark,
swooped with floured hands to a hot griddle – cooking soda bread
in heavy, fragrant slices soaked, by us, with salted butter
sweet and hot to taste,
while a kettle rested on the black
fussing and whistling in a permanent boil.
But my strongest memory – and one of nurturing love –
was of coming home from school when I was young.
On winter days, we'd tumble in the door – socks dirty,
mouths agape like quarrelling hungry birds –
to where our mother would be waiting, eyes bright with our return,
to set us at the table one by one.
The range door opened with a searing blast
and out came hand-made pancakes, hot and crisp and sweet.
Placed there before we'd walked up home,
the stacks of honey discs shimmered like a mirage,
glossy with butter, sprinkled with sugar, light as a sleeping kiss.
Each bite was a scalding heaven.

We'd bite, howl, chew then howl again,
but plates were emptied, and forks sucked clean.
I still remember those pancake days –
three small girls clustered around a table cooing happily like doves.
And making sure we had all that we needed,
my mother, flushed with happiness, heat and love.

WALKING HOME FROM SCHOOL

We walked the last mile home each day;
three small girls, satchelled; often scratched
from playground races and farmyard games.

In spring, the hedges burst with flowers;
bluebells rippled past us down the steepest banks
while we drew sweetness from the primrose hearts
and stitchwort laced our way.

I walk the road, now, on some quiet afternoons,
and visit trees – now aged and tall –
that we once jumped from; played around.

And sometimes, if the day is true,
I press my face against the weathered, gnarled bark
and hear childish voices, still.

THIS PAGE

No boundaries mark this open page,
yet, on the broad-horizoned land,
fields, mended hedges, broken walls
mark exactly where I may not go.

A page – this page – is open to the sky.

Times past, on snowy winter days
three small girls slid, shrieking, down a snowy hill.
Boundaries were a whispered dare,
a looming thrill.
Only a final curve – and a moment where we
leapt for safety moments before disaster –
drove us deep into snow,
not pinioned on leafless briars
beneath the cold barbed wire.

We raced through crop-filled summer fields,
picked raspberries and blackberries,
sweetening our lips and nights
tasting summer and autumn on our tongue.

Later we found ourselves older. Worn.
Drawn inexorably to the edge of things.
Moving towards the boundaries of the day.

Keep the book. Open the page.
This page – this page – is open to the sky.

NOTES OF A YEAR

January:
Bitter winds scrape against the hour of a late January day like metal over bone.
Winter is the time for wounds to rise; for clotted scars to twist their way across the people and their land.

February:
An icy dusk presses in against my skin. Where I stand on this frozen ground, only the gentle colour of birdsong connects me to the day

March:
Dawn breaks quietly over land, long-worked and known well. It is nature that tells us the time in the hedgerows and the sky.

April:
The hedges sing in spring, calling summer to the door. Now mist moves in, slow as an afternoon thought. Little by little, sounds of the day begin to settle, clinging close and low to the land.

May:
In the glow of evening light, small birds feed. I read their movements as I would the notations of a song. A delicate hymn. Graceful music fallen from a glowing sky.

June:
Above the fields which are rich and ripe and full, I find the midnight sky. A golden glow will rest along the horizon's edge until the sun returns.

July:
I have summer in my bones and heat on my skin. This morning light is a gentle voice at my window that calls me out to meet the day.

August:
I make my way to the river. Gentle, late light and a softness in the air. Birdsong flows like water before me.

September:
Starlight pierces the branches of September trees. I look up and remember what wheels above me. Here is my place. My space.

October.
This light that falls across the land carries us towards the bridge of the year and draws us safely to the other side.

November.
This is a time to find texture, age and line. Winter lays bare its slow, silent beauty in the hedgerows around the farm.

December.
December days are empty of leaf and light and song. We must seek our winter fire in the heart, the hearth, the sky.

THE CALL (FOR AVA)

There is something timeless
in giving voice this summer night.
Calling, I step out into the yard
through a settling dusk
to bring the small cat home.

She has dozed peacefully this summer day,
drawing down the sun into her thick, dark fur
and now the coolness of the night has set her free.

I call again. Turn to read growing shadows.
Wait for darkness to step out beyond darkness.
For the unformed to become form.

She will be all small paws, twitching ears and wide, bright eyes.
Her coat prickled thick with burrs and seeds,
sweetened by flowers that gifted their scents to the still-warm air.
I will hear her voice, move to lift her into me
and breathe in her memory of a summer's day.

Quietly, I wait on the edge of night to call her home.

SEEDS

The farm was never silent. Daybreak
found my parents busy in the byres,
heavy buckets swinging lightly in my father's hands
as my mother gathered eggs and scattered grain.
Pigs grumbled low into the morning
and chickens scrambled, scolding, towards the light.
Young calves frothed themselves in milk
while heifers (sensing spring) shifted, restless, in their pens.

We knew the sound of tractors starting up
and moving through the yard. Cars coming
to the house brought cattle dealers, men
from grain mills, the breadman on a Wednesday,
visits from family, sometimes – if necessary –
a call from the vet, the traveller who sold
my mother roller towels, the minister twice a year
(or less if the dog was in the yard).

And now they hang, those precious sounds,
as moments suspended on the edge of loss.
Fragile as a heavy-seeded grass, midsummer-full.
One by one, those memories echo through the empty farm
and, as the wind rises on a fresh cool day,
that grass is drawn up into the breeze
and all the precious seeds
so delicate,
so far beyond our grasp,
are scattered now
and gone.

BE THANKFUL TO THE DAY

(after ee cummings)

be thankful to the day
this precious here
this captured moment now
a place of light and loveliness
my tiny corner so bereft of morning breeze
and warmed by slowly gathering sun
for this morning I am seeker, mixer,
chalice-bearer,
the careful, slow taster of coffee freshly brewed
so sweetly now and dark and strong
this golden promised day
and I am grateful to be filled with senses
tipped generously open, wide,
to the light, bright chatter of new-morning birds
while beneath the endless arch of a cathedral sky
I rest this weight of bones
of known, warmed flesh
and lived-in skin
that shapes me
on this worn spring bench
that brings me to
this perfect morning
and this moment
now

THE OLD STONE WALL

So much is lost.
I walk the lane this slow and silent night
up towards an old out-farm.
A soft mist curls low on empty mossy fields
and the patient wildflower scent is strong.
Three small girls – a trio of unruly ghosts –
tumble behind me as I go,
racing past me up the summer lane
to find their father at the hay,
chasing a small dog, yelping, laughing,
carrying a bottle of tea and a wrapped piece for the hungry man.

I see them walking behind the trailer on an autumn dusk
hair prickling with flecks of straw
mouths sweet and dark with berries
plucked warm from a September hedge.

I find them huddled, golden-eyed and still, on a dark October night
watching bonfire sparks burst up into the stars,
their peach-soft faces blushed with heat
each goose-bumped with terror of the encroaching night.

The lands and farm are done.
Sold on, re-worked, the houses razed.
Only a worn stone wall – aged older than the girls – remains.
We climbed it then –
knew it simply as a barrier rough and tall –
a challenge to our brief-lived years.
Tonight, I see it as a thing of timeless beauty.
A tale of workmanship and pride.

Three small girls tumble over it
riotous and laughing
and are gone.

SUMMER 5.06AM

Dawn runs careless fingers
gently over the lip of the horizon –
soft and slow, like a young girl
trailing her hand
through still, dark water.
And, like ripples rising
to the surface of the day,
the light begins.

EVERYTHING, IT SEEMS, CONTAINS SONGS.

Music is layered everywhere.
A man places a slice
of a tree trunk on to a record player
and draws the needle down.
Chords, striving for harmony,
play the music held inside the tree.
Jupiter's charged particles sing across
its magnetosphere, while electrons spiral
in an endless chorus of waves
from Earth's Van Allen radiation belts.

Planets and stars pulsate in similar wavelengths –
electromagnetic songs of nameless moons.

An almost imperceptible hum
emanates from earth's
perpetually rolling atmosphere
in ring-shaped oscillations,
while the pulse of long ocean waves
breaks in concert over steep continental shelves
and shifting seismic plates.

Voyager once moved out – and through –
vibrations of interstellar plasma,
carried on a dark wave of song.
The sun's coronal loops vibrate
transversely as a guitar
and longtitudinally as a wind instrument;
visual vibrations translated into sound.

Everything, it seems, contains songs.

How then can we not, as beings, sing?

THE WEDDING SHAWL

I'm told there is a shawl
so delicate and so infinitely beautiful
that it is crafted to be passed within
the golden beauty
of a single wedding ring.
So it is with summer – drawn through
the delicate opacity
of spring.

THE BRIDGE

Cycling to school,
I'd long for it.
I'd race to cross it.

Drawn through an ancient grove
of beech trees arcing in soft, green light,
I'd begin to smile. Pedalling faster
towards the long, slow curve and then a dip,
I'd make my final sweeping turn
towards the waiting bridge
then rush into the rise and the soaring lift.

A ten-year-old kid whooping her way
over a hump-backed bridge,
heart and wheels in flight.

Now, decades on,
I drive – don't cycle –
to the self-same bridge, still there.
Everything is safe now.
Homogenised.
The road is ironed flat.

How, then, can you explain
that the child in me
still races forward?
Still feels the lift – the leap –
the soaring flight
of a bridge long gone?

CORNCRAKE

No living bird, this,
but the shadowed fragment of a slate-like song
caught deep within a slight, half-span of honeyed wood.
One side carved in rolling curves – red hieroglyphs marking their ebb and flow –
the other, a broad straight edge
pressed smoothly warm into my father's palm.
Stepping through my soft-edged memory, now, he moves
bright-eyed and smiling, round the corner of the byre –
a jagged memory of that small, lost bird
borne carefully in his large, cupped hands
as he carries his gopen-ful[1] of sound.
He touches the wood gently with a shining metal arc –
bright and cool as a sickle-sharp winter moon –
and the rasping cry of a corncrake leaps between his fingers, sharpening our air.
Can you hear it?
His eyes meet mine and his smile is sweet.
Can you hear it?

This rough call echoed once around the fields
when men, long-ago, scythed grass then forked the hay
as horses, straining with each fragrant load
hauled sweet summer harvest to the shed.
When hedges rippled slowly in a lush kaleidoscope of green
and a lonely dog barked in the yard.
I hold this slip of wood and think of fields cropped warm and stubble-bare;
tilly lamps hissing in a clean, cool room
as men greet the woman of the house and lay their caps aside,
chairs pulled in to a table heavy with food and bread and tea.
Small children – my father and his sister – shadow quiet as voices flow.
A bisom[2] and a patient cat standing silent at the door,
while behind the house, the flint-like echo of a corncrake in the empty field.

---

[1] A means of measuring or holding a fixed amount using both hands cupped together.
[2] A long-handled straw broom.

Now my father's smile, so soft and clear in his aged, sun-browned face
as he gently offers the singing wood for me to try:
to give the corncrake voice again.
Can you hear it?

STARS

The frosted stars,
implacable beauty,
arch gently through the darkened sky
while I,
rooted here,
silent as a glittering orb,
shine in reply.

RELAY

October races towards November, still like a child at play.
November reaches slowly down and takes its toy away.

LIKE WATER OVER STONE

Sometimes love is like water over stone.
The memories we have gathered up and made our own
lie quiet and still like small, cool pebbles
in our cupped palms.
Then love, like water, trickling clear across our skin,
washes the surface of each precious moment,
eases into every nook and cranny
and fills the spaces that we cannot see.

MOON SHADOW

As the moon rests easy in an April sky,
I watch it balance on its very tip
as a slight, pale curve rising up the blue.
A sure sign – as my father told me once –
that it will rain.

But not just yet.

Beneath it, dipping shyly behind
the soft pink clouds of evening
I find a star.

In that moment, I am climbing
a worn iron gate,
to stand, our heads together, with my father
as we look up into an endless winter sky.
We are not far beyond the comfort of the low-lit yard,
but night has claimed us here.

There is dark and there is darkness.
Low hills, bundled close behind the farm,
bring a stillness and a depth to the horizon.
A lack of stars. A sense of something solid.
A distance to be reached.
To be moved beyond.

Now, decades older,
I turn again to watch the evening sky
and, in the shadow of the moon,
remember that small child
reaching to the stars.

CAT (FOR OEDIE)

The old blind cat
sits quietly
on the windowsill,
pressing his face
carefully
against cool morning glass
as he listens to summer
scampering past him
like a kitten.

A QUIET MAN

He was a quiet man, always,
a second brother and a younger son.
He'd lost two fingers in his youth - an accident at home –
yet played piano every Sabbath in the Mission Hall,
dedicating himself afresh each time to Christ.
Late in life, love and a lady brought him to our summer road.
He stepped out with her into the evening's lazy light,
knew her compact and neat with a stillness like his own,
felt his broken hand held softly by this girl who would be his wife.
Our neighbours smiled to see them walking there,
quietly relieved he would not remain alone.
Later, he'd walk the road stripped clean of summer,
his gaze bent dark and low against the encroaching cold,
hands driven deep into winter pockets
while his sick wife waited, pale, inside their car.
He'd return to her with gifts beyond their season;
colour culled from hedgerows - wistful promises of life –
late roses stilled by frost clasped tightly in his damaged hand.
She'd smile and hold them close against her fading skin
pretending, still, to have a sense of smell.

When she died, he did not walk the road again.

These winter nights, I still think of him,
imagining beyond what townsfolk later said
of his last moments on that empty night
as he stood, already wraith-like, by the harbour wall
and struggled, with his injured hand, to close his jacket,
to button right to the top - for habit's sake, not heat –
before he stepped into the water
and was gone.

MORNINGS IN AUTUMN

Mornings in autumn
catch the quiet beauty of the year.
Small roads once filled with grass and flowers
echo with sudden silence now.
Only the clacking of magpies,
the rough-sawn caws of rooks
and the liquid beauty of fading birdsong remain.

Somewhere in the distance,
wood pigeons call softly to each other
and the key turns in the golden cage of morning.

I sit here – at peace.
Leave the door open.
The key may lie, hesitant, in the lock;
I will not try to leave.

HAME

The sound of childhood mornings.
My mother shaking out the grieshochs in the range
as light spills into the kitchen like an early guest
and the day gets underway.

I sit at the same old table now and feel the day begin.
Stirring this memory of language, buried things slowly rise.

Dreich winter morarnins kepping beasts as a wean.
Scunnered. Foundered to the bone.
Dumping barrowloads of pig shite in the midden,
cowping the wheelbarrow at an angle,
careful not to get japped wi' burning specks of dung.

Aulder now. Clabbered to the oxters. Wellingtons thick wi'
muck and glar. Hefting a new-born calf across a winter field –
it rescued from a sheugh and drooonin' in the watter –
I cairry this foundered wee beast, slippery, stairvin' and near still,
heavy in my airms
while its mither, wile wi' fright, loses the head and gives chase.
Wild and wake, head low, guldering frae her throat
skitin' an' high-steppin' through the mud intae madness.

This living tongue was one I once misplaced.
Moving out into the world, I withdrew from it. Laid it by.
Now I am ready to taste these words again.
Set them loose upon my tongue.
This newly remembered voice.
My coming home.

ICE STORM

The coldness calls. I step
into an exhalation of the night.
In this moon-blue silence
taut as wire, branches glitter still
or crack like something sudden fallen dark.
I raise my face --
a small pale moon.
I open my arms, these acres, wide.
I inhale the waiting stars.

THE COAT

This morning, I found
the coat you used to wear
around the farm.
A mongrel of a thing –
heavy, rough and strong.
I move to touch it
with careful fingers,
reading my history of you
like braille within the cloth.

HUNGER

Heads pressed low like cattle walking into rain,
we ploughed into the bleak November dusk,
following our father as he strode into the dark.
The cattle that he checked each winter's night
moved slowly through the sloping, generous field.

Once full of rich sward with thickened green –
a bowl for a still, hot summer sun –
it now lay scuffed and bare as it emptied with the year.
Winds whistled through desolate hedges,
hulking low and beast-like
in the darkest corners of the field before lifting to the sky.

We knew this sound for what it was – had grown with it –
but we remained aloof: buckling down our fear
like strapping a satchel closed on an unwelcome task.
It was the phone lines –
taut as webbing in that bitter, threatening sky –
that caught our imaginations then set all scrambling free
like mindless, scuttering frenzied things.

Plucked by a prowling breeze, the lines began to hum.
A howling chorus of voices that soared within the wind –
seeming to echo the approach of some unholy things.
This was the voice of lost and lonely souls
caught high in the web of night.
A ravenous legion that capered madly above,
seeking to fall upon us and then take their fill.
We recognised the sounds of hunger – and we ran.

I remember turning from my father in that night-time field
to race, dry-mouthed, in pistoning, thick, fat steps for home,
the heavy rubber of my muddied boots
slapping against my calves as I shrieked and ran.
Three small girls raced each other
to outrun the siren song.
We sped towards light, towards safety,
towards what we knew.
The night closed fast and low behind us –
hungry, dark, unfed.

BURIAL OF A FARM DOG

The dog had reached
his time
or past his time.
I quietly walk
the length and breadth
of land for him.
Then, weeping, dig.

THE SUMMER CLOCK

If she could have her way, she said,
she would have liked to own a summer clock.
A gleaming, simple timepiece
to gather hours – not mark their passing –
placed snugly in a corner of the room.

It would reach out, take hold, of summer time, she said,
capturing the sun-spun moments of light each day,
keeping away the long, dark winter hours.
And there would be a corner of her house
that would remain afire.

She said this in a wistful tone, soft as a dawn,
then turned her hopeful gaze to me.
But in seeing, she looked far beyond me, then,
into the lowering darkness of an October day.

IF

That my father would step
into this precious morning,
closing my grief
behind him like a gate
to stand here, quietly,
at the farm with me.

I would draw him close,
talking of harvests and crop-filled sheds,
of animals fed for the evening,
sharing my memory of a man climbing with ease
above the raised bars in the byre
while his small daughters
shrieked in delight.

I would tell him of my quiet love, too,
in our final long, slow days
and of his fingers stroking mine
– much smaller, then, cupped safely in his palm --
as we sat together
those quiet Sunday mornings
in the family pew.

THE PAINTING OF A COUNTRY SKY

I am not needed here to make this beautiful.
This summer day now moving through the softest wash
of cloud into the dusk of evening has no need of me.
I stand, regardless, to watch time fall away
while the sun gathers these moments in fading colour,
tucking them into a soft horizon that has become
a seamless transition between the day that has been
and the night that is to come.

MEMORY (A FRAGMENT)

You walk the fields here, or the hedges,
lift the gates or balance at the top,
swinging your weight along your leg
to pivot, stretch and jump back down.

These home fields filled our summer days.
We ran them, chased the dog, hauled back straying beasts.
Later, I learned to work them; I cropped and tilled,
birthed young calves, baled hay and straw.

My strongest memory
is standing quietly without hope where four fields met
high on a hill, protected by a brittle whitethorn hedge
with dry stone walls converging at a silent well.

My father, kneeling, weeping, beside a dying cow,
his calloused hands gentle on her straining neck,
her head on his lap,
her cold eyes towards the empty sky.

DERELICTION

There is more than lifting stones to do
though that itself is task enough.
The years bring slippage with them.
Old byres still stand
but out of focus now.
A blurring at the edges.
A softening of focus.

Strange that stone should soften somehow.
Strange that dereliction
should be so beautiful
so patient, so steady
and so complete.

TRIOLET FOR MY FATHER

I live on the old farm where I grew up with my parents and my sisters. My father would often walk up the road to check the cattle that were out in nearby fields and I'd sit on the wall in front of the farmhouse to watch him walk back down the road towards home. I knew, even when I was young, that I'd have to store such precious memories away. One day the road would be empty.

I watch my father as he walks the road
and memorise each step he takes.
I need to remember how he strode.
I watch my father as he walks the road.
Later, as we walk, his pace is slowed.
I help him then. We share the load.
I watch my father as he walks the road
and memorise each step he takes.

DREAM

Tonight,
wishes fill the sky like stars
and we, the dreamers,
stand between
the planets and the soil.

BAPTISM AT THE FARM WELL

Summer has come gradually to its knees.
The year is wearing thin now. It is growing tired and slow.
Darkness and memory slipping ever closer to the edges of the day.
On this soft blue night, in one final patient dusk, I feel the year begin to falter.
I have come to stand alone here beside the river's edge,
drawn by the sound of running water,
my face raised to the memory of a distant summer day.

I am twelve years old and, with my father, making hay.
Once morning-eager with the promise of my long-grown bones,
muscles taut and strong under my salt-slick skin,
I have hefted a summer-full of grass within these the scented hours
and I am weary now.

My father calls me to the brow of the hill where four fields meet.
It is a small, dark copse. A shaded spot.
And there, silent, still, together,
my eyes raised beyond the summer branches to an open sky,
a sky that soars, unvaulted, into the blue,
my father reaches into the well his family once searched and found –
water centuries cool and shadowed now –
and baptizes me in the water of the day.

This is the correct order of my heart. This life. This moment.
The water trickles down my sun-scorched skin and I am elemental.
Water. Air. Soil. Sky. Sun. Growth within me and around me.
I will flourish here. Blessed and baptized this golden summer day.

Now my eyes are open, and the sun is gone.
There is a depth beyond silence and the shape of words.
A gentle movement in the water that I mistake, almost, for a breeze.

Will you join me here?
Feel the weight, the movement
and the benediction of the water and the sky?
Stand beside me as the stars catch fire?

AUTUMN MANUSCRIPT

Minims and crotchets
of hungry black crows
on shorn autumn fields
rewriting the music of the season
as they rise and swoop and fall.

LIGHT; THE OLD FARM

These are the days when the light moves slowly on.
When summer, wrapped up gently as any precious gift,
ebbs slowly – and, in leaving us, seems sweeter than before.
I search for beauty in the fields around the farm
and find berry-clustered hedges, limned in leaf of gold,
glowing brightly, still-life like, rich with colour,
holding the weight – if not the heat – of the lowering sun.
For autumn light brings with it a fading memory of warmth
and falls in layers of stillness now – a slow retreat –
pressing more lightly in against the shortening day.
These days I carry close to me, as something treasured,
my memories of this farm on a clear summer's day.
Dawn brought with it, then, rich promises of toil.
Unwrapped in soft blue mornings, filigreed with mist,
thick swathes of grass, falling freshly-mown behind my father's blades,
dried, crisp and fragrant, under a golden sun.
We carried light within us – in childish voices and in laughter –
from fields to kitchen, then racing back outdoors:
each voice, a note of busy happiness we did not know we sang.
Later, in the room we shared, folded and tucked in tight,
summer light pooling in golden shadows at the foot of each small bed,
mist softening, again, the edges of the glorious day,
roads, hedges, cattle, cats still warm with the memory of sun,
and a waterfall of birdsong echoing through the falling dusk.
The fading light of autumn, now, is a different, sombre thing.
The yard is stilled; old houses empty, tractors gone.
The choir of birds is silenced too. Some have already flown.
Those remaining have withdrawn from the immediacy of the day.
Leaves are weighted now and still, caught on the cusp of colour, waiting to fall.
Only shadows fill the quiet, lonely byres.
The pale light of winter will be a barren gift –
something to yearn for and yet lose too soon.
Such meagre light will prove a mere echo of the generous summer sun
and will not fill the faltering heart or thaw the frozen soil.

The frosted light draws out, instead, the scents and sounds of a fading year;
the sweetened smoke of peat fires fragrance the still, cool air,
and in the icy, lowering darkness a fox's bark echoes
harshly across the empty, frozen fields
while glittering stars burn cold
and the old farm lies quiet and still.

THE GIFT

You lift a human heart, he told me, as you would a leaf,
gently and with care; your fingers cupped
beneath their stillness, for they may break in their fragility
and crumble at your well-intentioned charge.
We bear our seasons deep within us –
shadowed summers and bright winter days –
but there are autumn moments all too often
that weaken us and bring us low.

A simple thought – a moment of awareness –
is all it takes to lift a failing heart.
And there is beauty in such quiet consideration
when we can know that we have played our part.

SHADOW CLOUD STONE

Such an adventure it was to climb the hill and scan the land below,
looking for passing shadows on a summer's day.
Searching the sward for clouds caught between earth and sun
that would set darkness free to race across the fields before us –
huge shadows billowing like souls released –
rippling wild over earth and grass and stone.

We'd stand there – three small girls – blushing with summer heat,
raising our heads to the coolness passing over us,
sensing the shadows fly.

As I grew, my father told me of a seamstress
who'd lived outside a tiny hamlet not so far from here.
She worked her needle deftly; took in mending,
sewed shirts for all and sundry.
Kept a small garden, two chickens and a goat.
Walked her way to services twice each Sabbath.
Never married. Lived alone.

No house remains.
Only a bramble-scuffed path and crumbling stones
mark where a life was lived.
She is a summer cloud shadow, now,
drifting across the land.

Nothing remains when we look into the sun.

SONG

Pick each bud
like a note from
the blossoming hedge,
and welcome
the chorus of spring.

STONE

With death, after snaps at the heels
of what went before.
A forced line of demarcation drives me on
till what I am is both old and new in one.

I am scattered now as soil.
Broken as weathered stone.
I have searched through nature for the thing
that will fit the new shape of my heart.

I was once a winter fire.
A soft, slow rain in spring.
The flat heat of a generous summer sun.
Autumn silvered with dawn.

Now I have become the broken walls of these old byres
shadowed by memories of task and toil.
I am darkening windows lit by a faint moon.
I am the gathered stories of a forgotten home.

I am a weighted boulder,
set low and heavy on the riverbed.
No flood will move me on.

I am our days and my own in one.

THE OLD FARMER

He is patient as the routine of the day begins –
silent and considered as a cobweb in the morning sun.
The sounds around him are familiar to him now:
the truck door clumping shut as his brother –
another old man taut and spare – steps out to greet a farming friend
in a conversation that is little more than light and shade.
A murmuration of words that
swoop and whisper round the corners of the vehicle
to rise untrammelled into the morning blue.

Sometimes, he remembers they are old.

Summers and unrelenting time have dried them through.
They are as husks now, light and golden this summer's day.
So much so that, with the slightest breath,
in a single moment, they might be lifted into the air and finally blown away.

A dog leans in against him, not so much for work these days,
yet still considered as though it pays its way.
A damp nose seeks his hand. He cups frail fingers. Feels the warm, damp
exhalation of the animal moving soft against his skin.

He is beyond this moment now, fallen into memories of working sheep in
summer.
His dog flickers like a shadow, long and low across the billowing grass,
honeyed dark eyes glancing from him to the skittish animals and back again,
drawn like a second thought across the field.

Voices raised in laughter scatter the past to shadow
just for a moment, but they are little more than ghosts
beyond the old truck and the quiet man held within.
The dog shifts slightly, lying warm against rough fabric
pushed high by bony knees as the old man strokes his patient head.

The man looks down, seeing hands that are now more bone than living flesh,
marked by scars and darkening spots that bloom with age.

Inside his bones and weathered skin, he is a young boy
walking across the early light of a morning field, dog by his heels.
The old man lays his head against the cool glass of the window,
closes his eyes and dreams of a summer day.

SUMMER HAIKU

Summer morning light
will slip, like the finest yarn,
through the tightest grasp.

WHAT WE HAVE IS THIS

Earth will tell the time. As will
the small, bright birds who call this morning to attention,
rising as flames from a newly ignited sun.
These days, we stumble into unfamiliar mornings
where we sense each passing shadow
and find within us where the light falls clean.

This other natural time has always run beside our busy lives –
a quieter flow that seeped beneath our skin.
We feel it now; become aware of its incessant pull.
Discern the powerful swell that draws us swiftly on.

We have returned to nature now – to water, air and light –
as our voraciously demanding world has fallen away.
Given the chance to understand –
in this time of silence and of knowing --
what has always been.

These birds.
This air.
Ourselves.
This morning sun.

THE GOLDEN ROOM

As the evenings begin to darken and draw down,
I will slip quietly to work inside this golden room.
My burgeoning joy is twofold:
in catching memories and in finding light.

Early in the morning,
this tiny space is densely shadowed; nothing more.
But a west-facing window
draws the evening sun towards it like a song.
In precious moments, then,
caught on the silent tipping-point of dusk,
the walls of this tiny space are set aglow,
lifting my heart each time with fresh surprise and joy.

It was a small and plain bedroom once.
My mother brought us here when we were born;
three tiny girls drawing new light into her days.
We lay heart-close with her in those peaceful early nights
while she held the children she thought she'd never have.

I feel her sometimes, with me, here,
as I open the door and walk into this evening-silent space,
sensing a light inexorably drawn into this gentle, golden room.
I imagine her, bathed in peaceful sunlight
as she holds me, singing softly,
watching my narrow chest rise and fall.
My tiny fingers held carefully in hers.

SHADOW FOLK

Some future season when
the autumn night is bright
and full and still, we
will – in one pure moment,
pierced in equal measure by
both pain and joy – come
to see ourselves as we will be
remembered here: cool,
dark shadows lying moon-quiet against
the surface of a still-warm soil.

END OF YEAR

From here, you can see the fabric of the year
scuffed raw and worn thin
around a grey horizon's fine and unforgiving rim.
Today, the sun is light and empty; nothing more.
Sudden gusts of desolate, bitter wind
busy themselves along the weakening edges of the moment,
delving in, seeking to loosen, then to pry
all that holds them from the remnants of the day.
The desiccated husks of time
are borne up, gossamer-thin, translucent,
rising loose in tattered fragments
towards an abandoned sky.

THE DARK

It isn't dark, this house, she says,
and runs her hands
down peeling whitewashed walls,
still smoothly luminous
this silent moonlit night.
Walk me down the yard, she says,
place me anywhere,
and though the night be black as pitch,
I will find my way.

She sits outdoors, these quiet nights,
back straight against the scuffed door.
A patient shadow,
dwarfed by the empty house behind her.
A solitary figure now.
Face raised happily to late summer stars,
remembering what used to be.

THE LETTING GO

According to research, memories are stored in the prefrontal, medial temporal and parietal cortices – the last parts of the brain that continue to function when we get close to death. Charon's obol – or stone – is an allusive term for the coin placed in or on the mouth of a dead person before burial – a payment or bribe for Charon the Ferryman who conveys souls across the river Styx.
I imagine these last moments as a kaleidoscope – no linear progression, no time limits. A lifetime of fragmented memories.

One: standing in the moss, bending to dip and lift morning water into my cupped palm, I let the cool blessing run across my skin.

Two: Walking in the spring, I seek out the haze of bluebells and, in the finding of them, come to understand that I have heard the opening notes of a familiar song.

Three: Cow sheds blossom with remembered light. My father balances himself over raised bars in the byre, his three small daughters shrieking with delight.

Four: Taking my hand, my mother steps beside me from the scullery door – light spilling across the first tight frost of the season. Standing together – then leaning back – we look up to feel the planet spin away from us as we rise into the endless arc of a winter sky.

Five: On a quiet spring evening, orphaned and heavy with grief, I press my hand into the soil and feel the heartbeat of the land.

Six: Passing the Donegal hills on a quiet morning train, I watch soft colours bruising the edges of the sky like fingers drawn through oil.

Seven: Older now, I stand within the slow exhalation of a summer night – while wild August roses cascade around me like the notes of a song.

It is a fine thing to craft words upon the page. To feel the weight of spoken vowels like river stones smooth at rest beneath my tongue.

I take these stones – these moments – from my mouth. Place them in the riverbed. Watch the water run clear.

ROSEHILL

One day, as roses bloom here, I will let you know
how this slow understanding of becoming
spread across my skin and moved within me
as something gradual – easing slow –
to warm my bones like the morning summer sun.
For I came to know that I was happy here.

I found peace waiting for me.
I sought the light and found it; let it in.

WALKING OFF THE LAND

Each time, we gather at the farm, like wingless crows
in darkly clustered groups - our faces solemn and still
against the background of a late spring day --
the season more piercing for being generous and fair.

The first year, I hold my father's hand,
guiding him gently behind the slowly walking men,
noting absently how their long, strong fingers
press in so tight and hard against each other's shoulders;
a gesture that, at any other time,
would have had me think of casual friendship.
Today, it is a generous and precious ritual
that calls me to the edge of tears.
Respect and quiet kindness in each silent lift.

The following year, my sister holds my arm
as we turn our backs upon the empty house
and step out into the day.

The assembled mourners walk behind us,
moving through blossoming light that is rich and warm and full;
sun shadowing steps that are heavy with love and grief and loss.
This is the final walk - the leaving of the farm -
precious moments recalled in each quiet step.
A journeyed generation of those who have lived this land.

Holy as any Sabbath, steeped in the history of our soil,
This, our walking off the land. A coffin, carried with love and grace
to the edge of fields a farmer and his family worked and owned.
Wise men know they do not own the land they love,
but belong, in turn, to summer hedges, October morning mists,
sun-warmed soil, graceful hares running lightly over a spring field,
winter stars above the darkening land, the myriad beauties of a farming life.

This walk is love. A shared memory of our miraculous days.
Our dusks and dawns. Our precious lives.
Soil in our veins. All else is past and still.

Quietly, and with love, we walk each coffin off the land.

MEMENTO MORI

I kept my mother's work clothes when she died.
The farming ones she wore through sun and rain.
And dreamed – as children hope and adults never do –
that she'd come back to wear them once again.

ACKNOWLEDGEMENTS:

With grateful thanks to: Arts Council of Northern Ireland for SIAP funding and continual support, the wonderful Kerry Buchanan, farmers (of all ages) for stories and memories, the patient Mark Davidson at Hedgehog Poetry Press and Garvagh Community Building for space, craic and kindness.